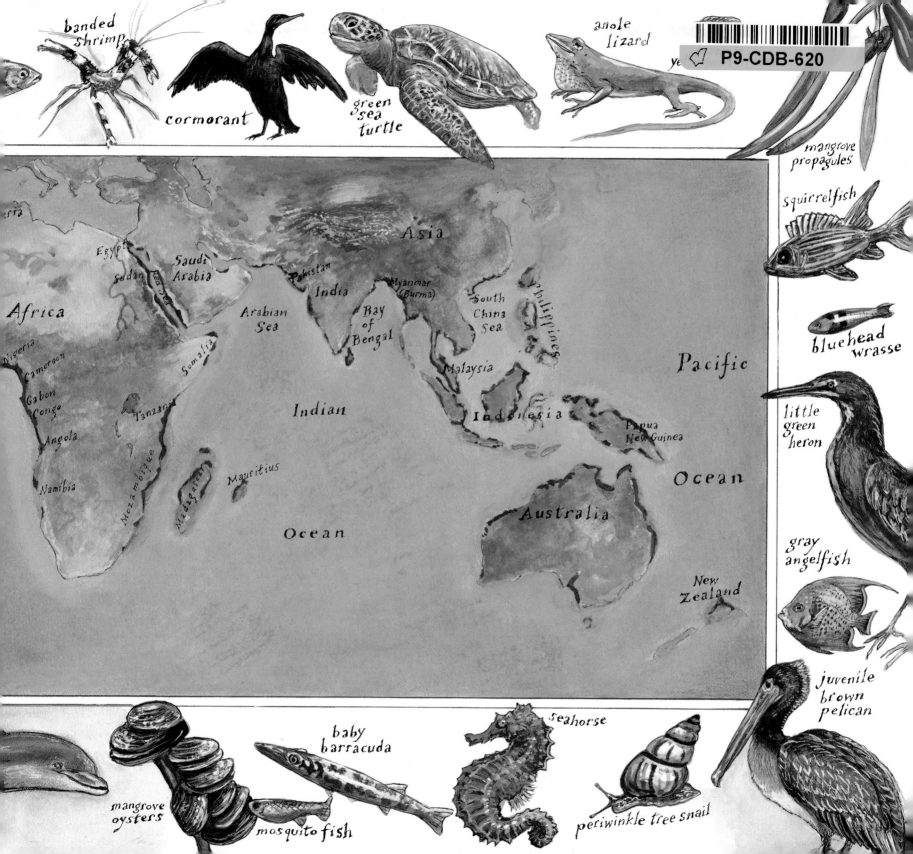

banded shrimp

cormorant

green sea turtle

anole lizard

P9-CDB-620

mangrove propagules

Squirrelfish

bluehead wrasse

little green heron

gray angelfish

juvenile brown pelican

Africa
Nigeria
Cameroon
Gabon
Congo
Angola
Namibia
Egypt
Sudan
Saudi Arabia
Red Sea
Somalia
Tanzania
Mozambique
Madagascar
Mauritius
Pakistan
India
Arabian Sea
Bay of Bengal
Myanmar (Burma)
Asia
South China Sea
Philippines
Malaysia
Indonesia
Papua New Guinea
Australia
New Zealand
Indian Ocean
Pacific Ocean

mangrove oysters

mosquito fish

baby barracuda

seahorse

periwinkle tree snail

With love to all the Cherrys, my loving, supportive, wonderful family:
Mom (Helen), Steve, Dawn, Jason, Lauren, Nicholas, Michael, Tracy, Cameron, and Ben

Introduction

The tropical sun warms the Caribbean lagoons all year round. Lagoons provide a perfect place for mangroves to take root. As a mangrove tree grows, it provides an ideal home for many animals. The bigger and more complex a mangrove island becomes, the more animals come to live amid its tangled branches and roots. Mangrove leaves fall into the water, get caught in the roots, and provide food for many living things. They decompose into muck in which sea grass can grow. In turn, sea grass is a wonderful habitat for sea turtles, seahorses, and hundreds of species of fish. Colorful corals and sea anemones colonize the mangrove roots and create reefs nearby. Night herons, great blue herons, brown pelicans, and other fish eaters hunt for dinner in the shallows around the mangrove trees. Tropical storms come frequently, but mangroves buffer the mainland from their powerful winds. Many of the shrimp and fish we eat start their lives in these protected nurseries around mangrove islands. This is the story of a community of living things that depend upon a tangle of mangrove trees in the Caribbean Sea.

Although all of the creatures featured in this book could not be found in one particular area of mangroves, most of them can be found in the mangroves of Belize; St. John, U.S. Virgin Islands; and Biscayne Bay, Florida (for instance, there are no manatees in the Virgin Islands now).

Copyright © 2004 by Lynne Cherry
All rights reserved
Distributed in Canada by Douglas & McIntyre Ltd.
Printed and bound in the United States of America by Berryville Graphics
Designed by Barbara Grzeslo
First edition, 2004
10 9 8 7 6 5 4 3 2

www.fsgkidsbooks.com

Library of Congress Cataloging-in-Publication Data
Cherry, Lynne.
     The sea, the storm, and the mangrove tangle / Lynne Cherry.
         p. cm.
     Summary: A seed from a mangrove tree floats on the sea until it comes to rest on the shore of a faraway lagoon where, over time, it becomes a mangrove island that shelters many birds and animals, even during a hurricane.
     ISBN 13: 978-0-374-36482-3
     ISBN 10: 0-374-36482-6
     [1. Mangrove swamps—Fiction.   2. Marine animals—Fiction.   3. Ecology—Fiction.
4. Caribbean Area—Fiction.]   I. Title.

PZ7.C41995 Se 2004
[Fic]—dc21
                                                              2002029705

THE SEA, THE STORM, AND THE MANGROVE TANGLE

BY LYNNE CHERRY

Farrar Straus Giroux — New York

Over a shallow, salty tropical sea, a flock of pelicans flew around a mangrove island.

From the branches of this tangle of mangroves dangled long sprouting seeds called propagules.

As a pelican landed, it jostled a branch and a propagule fell into the sea. For weeks the propagule was carried by a strong current until it came to rest on the shore of a faraway lagoon.

There it took root, sprouted leaves, and began to grow.
For decades, in the hot Caribbean sun, as tides rose and fell,
it slowly grew and grew and sent out prop roots to help it stand.

By its fiftieth year, its vast network of roots anchored the little mangrove tree, allowing it to survive storms. It was now quite a distinctive tree.

A mangrove tree crab scuttled by and exclaimed, "How can a tree grow in this salty sea?" She climbed the seedling to eat its leaves and made the mangrove her home. Mangrove oysters, sea anemones, and a coral settled on the roots. Small fiddler crabs dashed and darted about below the high tide line and disappeared into holes under the mangrove's roots.

A periwinkle tree snail came upon the mangrove seedling and thought, "I can eat the algae that grow on these roots." So it stayed on to live there.

Mangrove leaves fell into the water, decomposed, and turned into muck. In this muck, sea grass began to grow.

Several more years passed and the mangrove tree
became larger, sending out more branches and prop roots. It
grew flowers that were pollinated by the wind.

Driftwood floating across the sea carried anole lizards to the mangrove tree. "We can eat the ants, mosquitoes, and other insects that crawl and fly over these flowers," they thought.

Hummingbirds hid their nests within the mangrove's tangled branches, while a caterpillar and the mangrove tree crab nibbled on its leaves.

After the mangrove flowers dropped their petals, propagules formed. These living seeds grew long and heavy until they fell down between the mangrove roots into the sea grass. There the new propagules began to grow.

A seahorse carried his babies in a pouch in his belly. "Here is a good place for my babies to hide," he thought, and gently released them into the sea-grass bed. Mama shrimp and fish laid their eggs there. Grunts and mangrove snappers fed in the sea grass at night and, during the day, hid from bigger fish among the mangrove roots.

The propagules grew into many mangroves. For seventy years this mangrove tangle grew and spread out farther and farther.

Dolphins found the water around the mangroves teeming with fish and decided to stay there.

Manatees came to feed in the sea grass, and they, too, made the waters around the mangroves their home.

A hundred years had passed since the first propagule planted itself here and the mangrove tangle had become a big mangrove island.

As a flock of pelicans dove for fish, two fishermen came by. One said, "Let's cut these mangroves down and create a shrimp farm."

The other fisherman replied, "But these mangroves are the only trees that can grow in the salty seawater. Many of the fish in the ocean start their lives in nurseries around these mangrove islands. If we destroy the mangroves, we destroy the fish which give us all life." And so they went out to sea and left the island in peace.

Two pelicans tucked themselves into the mangroves and thought, "Here we can build a nest and dive for fish." Herons came to hunt for shrimp, crabs, and small fish. A magnificent frigatebird puffed up his large red pouch to impress his mate.

One afternoon, a pelican flew to the mangrove island.
Breathlessly she cautioned, "Beware! Prepare! A storm brews!
A wild wind blows this way!" She called to the creatures of the
air, "Come hide deep within the tangled branches of the
mangroves."

The manatees lifted their noses in the air and sniffed. Yes,
there was that sweet damp scent of rain. On the horizon, they
saw, far away, plumes of rain descending from a raft of dark
clouds. A hurricane was on its way.

The seahorses called to the other creatures of the sea, "Come with us! Beneath the roots in the center of the mangroves we will be safe!"

So they swam, crawled, scurried, and slithered to the shelter
of the mangrove roots.

That evening, the breeze became a screaming tempest. Thick, dark, frothing clouds raced through the sky. "The hurricane is here!" the animals cried. Winds sang and moaned through the mangrove tangle, lashing, breaking, and tearing branches.

The birds held on, fighting the power of the hurricane throughout the night. Under the sea, the sand churned as huge waves tossed and turned the fish and seahorses, trying to rip the mangrove roots from their hold on the seafloor.

The next morning, all was still. The sun shone from behind retreating purple clouds. And a mangrove propagule floated away on the current.

The birds came out from the safety of the mangroves' damaged branches. The periwinkle tree snails timidly peeked out from their shells and looked around. The fish, the crabs, and the seahorses swam out from the protection of the mangrove roots. All were safe.

Meanwhile, the mangrove propagule
blown by the storm came to rest on the shore
of a faraway lagoon.

Ten years have passed. Dead bleached branches still tell the story of the hurricane. But new growth has sprouted from the mangroves' broken branches, and the mangrove island is even bigger, wider, and deeper.

Now, while pelicans dry their feathers, and dolphins jump, roll, and play in the waves, and manatees lazily loll in their sea-grass bed . . . while a heron hunts in the shallows and a hawk screeches . . .

. . . that mangrove propagule carried on the waves to a faraway lagoon has now grown into a little mangrove tree. And there it will continue to grow . . . and grow . . . and grow.

Author's Note

Mangroves are in danger. They are being cut down in order to create shrimp farms and commercial developments such as hotels and vacation homes. Miami Beach was a mangrove island before it was clear-cut for tourist development.

Without mangroves, coastal areas are battered by ferocious storms that cause flooding and erosion. Mangroves act as a filter: when pollutants run off the land from roads, parking lots, and agricultural areas, mangroves help to clean the water. Mangroves stop the silt that washes downriver after clear-cutting. They prevent the silt from covering up and smothering coral reefs, which themselves are in danger. And without this natural habitat, we will be depleting the ocean of fish, which the world depends on for food. Many river fish spend a large part of their lives in the ocean (they are called anadromous), so the cutting of mangroves can also affect people and animals who eat freshwater fish.

You can visit an intact mangrove habitat at Biscayne National Park in Florida or the Virgin Islands National Park at St. John, U.S. Virgin Islands.

You can help save mangroves by writing letters in support of preserving mangrove ecosystems and by not eating shrimp unless you know where they were raised. Unless they are labeled and advertised differently, shrimp bought in supermarkets or restaurants today were raised on a shrimp farm. Every time you eat one of these shrimp, you "cast a vote" for replacing mangroves with shrimp farms.

For more information about mangroves and how you can help save them, check the Web sites of the Industrial Shrimp Action Network (ISA Net) at *www.shrimpaction.org* and the Mangrove Action Project at *www.earthisland.org/map/index.htm*. ISA Net is an umbrella group that supports and encourages sustainable, responsible shrimp farming and wetlands conservation and spawns campaigns against irresponsible shrimp aquaculture.

Acknowledgments

I owe the scientific accuracy of this book to many people, but primarily to mangrove biologist Candy Feller of the Smithsonian Environmental Research Center, Edgewater, Maryland, and Gary Bremen of Biscayne National Park in Florida. For taking me out to the mangroves, thanks to Laurel Brannick of the Virgin Islands National Park; Joey de Martelly, Virgin Islands Environmental Research Station; and, again, Gary Bremen. For reference photographs, special thanks to Dr. Jiangang Luo, University of Miami, Florida; Gary Bremen; Candy Feller, for providing photographs, especially of the distinctive little mangrove tree; photographer Gary Braasch; Klaus Ruetzler, National Museum of Natural History (NMNH), Smithsonian Institution; photographer Steve Simonsen; and biologist Mandy Joye.

For artist-in-residencies while working on this book, thanks to John Kress, director, Botany Department of the NMNH, Smithsonian Institution; Ray Bradley, director, Geosciences Department, University of Massachusetts, Amherst; the Durfee Conservatory (and to Phil, Libby, James, and Claire O'Neill for taking care of Jasper and Rocky in Amherst); James McElfish, director, Sustainable Use of Land Program, Environmental Law Institute, Washington, D.C.; Simon Levin, director of the Center for Biocomplexity and Moffett Professor of Biology, Department of Ecology and Evolutionary Biology, Princeton University, Princeton, New Jersey; and Michael Bean, attorney, Environmental Defense Fund, Washington, D.C.

Thanks to biologist Tom Hollowell, Botany Department, NMNH, Smithsonian Institution, for reading the manuscript, and to his son, Ashley, whose illustration of a fish amid mangrove roots originally inspired me to write this book.

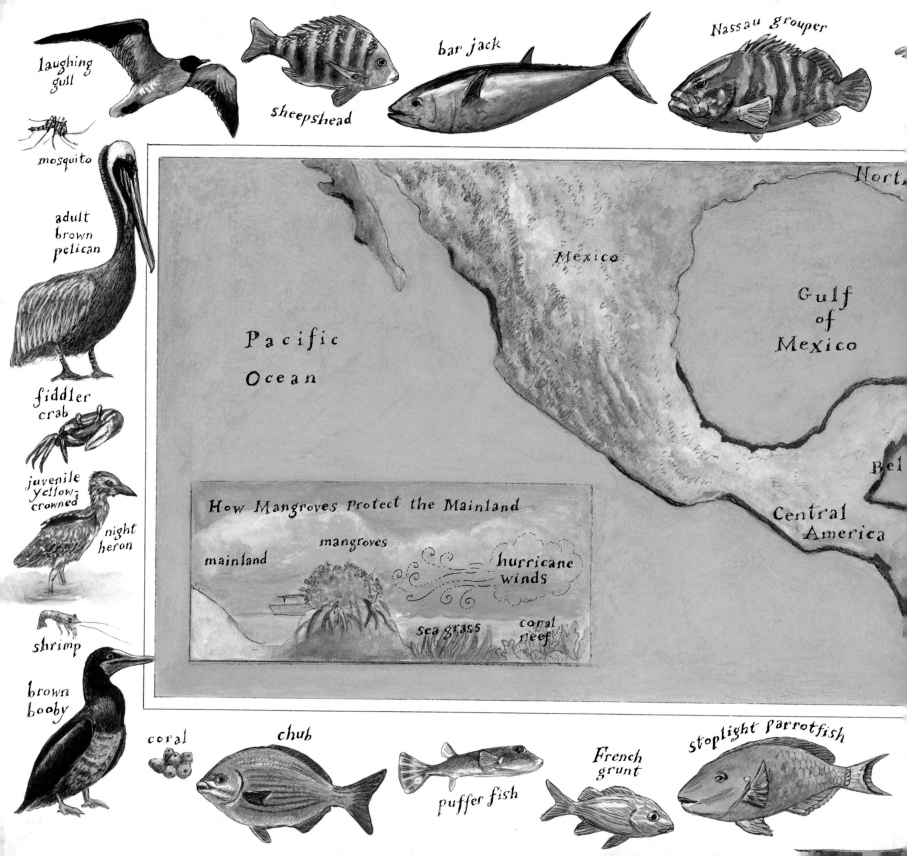

laughing
gull

mosquito

adult
brown
pelican

fiddler
crab

juvenile
yellow-
crowned

night
heron

shrimp

brown
booby

coral

chub

puffer fish

French
grunt

stoplight parrotfish

sheepshead

bar jack

Nassau grouper

Nort

Mexico

Pacific

Ocean

Gulf
of
Mexico

Bel

Central
America

How Mangroves Protect the Mainland

mainland

mangroves

hurricane
winds

sea grass

coral
reef